This Book Belongs To:

_____

1, 2, 3,

WHAT DO YOU SEE?

A Counting Book for Toddlers

First Rockridge Press trade hardcover edition 2022

Originally published in trade paperback by Rockridge Press 2021

For general information on our other products and services, please contact our Customer Care Department within the United States at (866) 744-2665, or outside the United States at (510) 253-0500.

Hardcover ISBN: 979-8-88608-487-0
Paperback ISBN: 978-1-64876-736-4
eBook ISBN: 978-1-64876-737-1

Manufactured in the United States of America

Interior and Cover Designer: Darren Samuel
Art Producer: Tom Hood
Editor: Laura Bryn Sisson
Production Manager: Martin Worthington
Production Editor: Melissa Edeburn

Photography © iStock, cover & pp 7, 12, 16, 19, 20, 28, 31, 32, 35, 36, 39, 40, 43, 44; Shutterstock, cover and pp 8, 11, 12, 15, 23, 24, 27.

10 9 8 7 6 5 4 3 2 1 0

Dear Reader,

Your toddler's brain is growing so fast that it's no wonder naptime is a welcome reprieve! By the time toddlers are 18 months old, they are learning one new word every two waking hours. Your little one is constantly absorbing new language and stimuli.

Studies show that although they don't have the words to express it, toddlers are able to understand numerical concepts, identify larger and smaller quantities, and even do some basic subtraction—all before they ask for more juice. Toddlers are hungry to learn new numbers and words. Here we've paired together the counting basics with photos of everyday objects your child will recognize and learn to label. You'll deepen your child's learning experience and expand their imagination, all while cherishing time spent together. Happy counting!

1

sleepy kitty

2

happy puppies

3

cuddly teddy bears

4
tough trucks

5

plastic sippy cups

6

cozy sweaters

7

squeaky ducks

8

bouncy balls

9

bright blocks

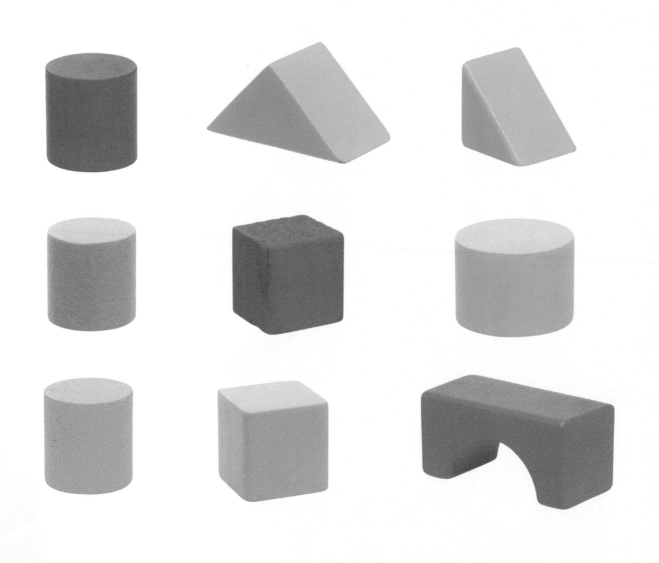

10
messy fingers

11
sticky donuts

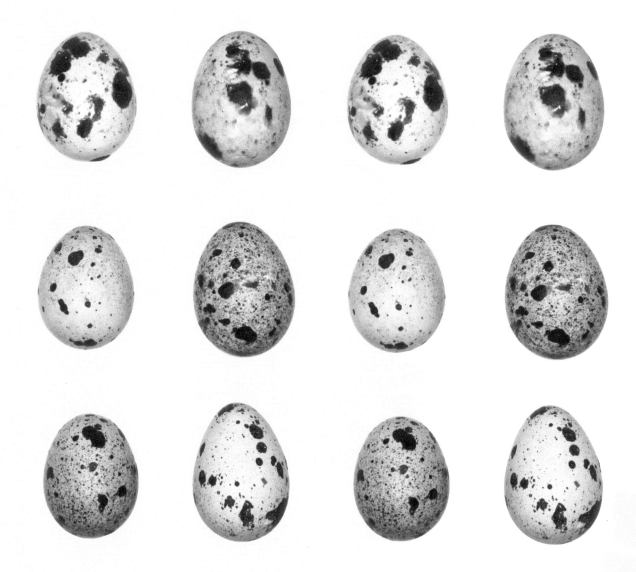

13

chewy cookies

12

speckled eggs

14

mini muffins

15

colorful crayons

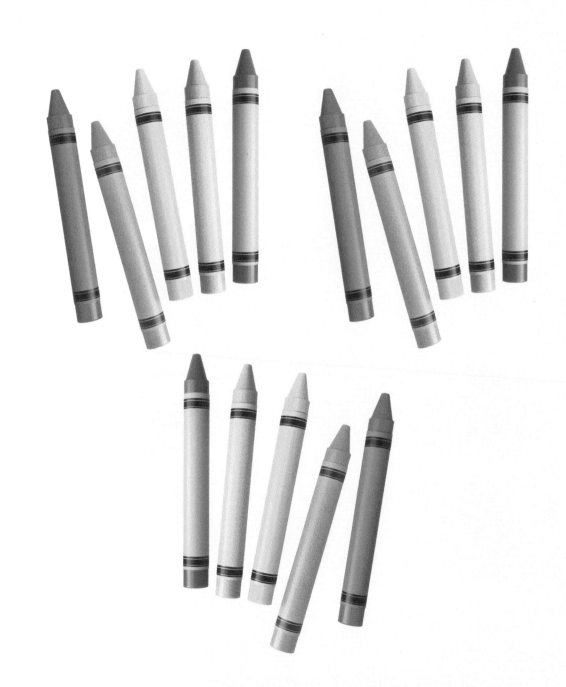

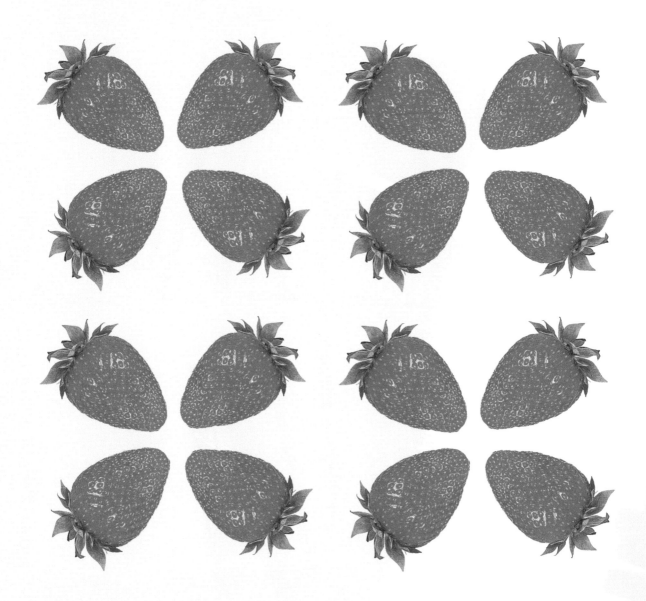

16
juicy berries

17
prickly
pine cones

18

crunchy leaves

19

plump acorns

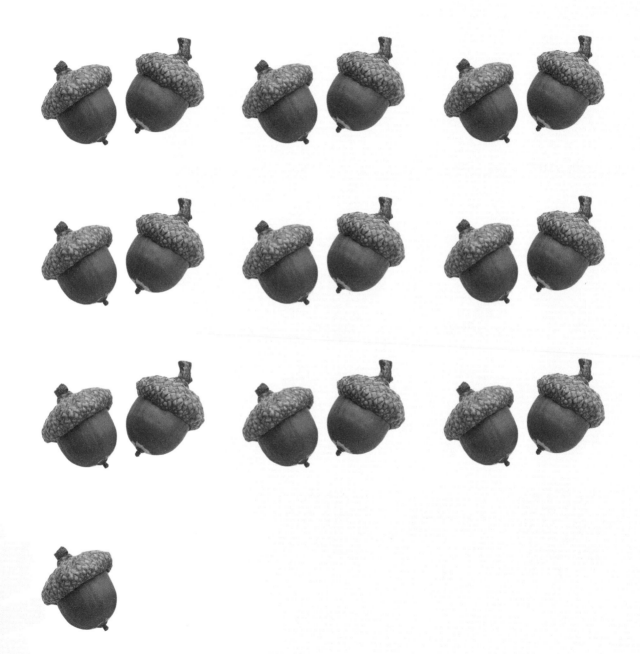

20

dainty flowers

Help reinforce what your toddler just learned with these fun counting activities to do together.

SCAVENGER HUNT

Practice counting with a scavenger hunt! Using the objects in this book as inspiration, see if your toddler can find some or all of the items on these pages. This activity can take place over an extended period of time.

Tip: Have your toddler find the object, rather than the corresponding number. For example, see how many blocks they can count in your living room, or how many strawberries you have in the refrigerator.

SQUISH PAINT ACTIVITY

Try counting with a fun sensory activity. Place 20 small dollops of paint on a blank sheet of paper. Carefully seal the page (while the paint is still wet) in a clear, zip-top plastic bag. Have your child "squish" each paint dot with their finger while they count from 1 to 20!

NUMBER MAT

Use a number mat to teach your toddler number identification! Collect small objects, like cereal pieces or pom-poms. On a sheet of paper, draw a grid with 20 boxes and number each box. To play, pick a number and have your child place a small object into each box, counting up to the number as they go. Move on to another number and repeat. When your child is ready, let them perform this activity without the boxes.

HOPSCOTCH NUMBER LINE

Turn counting into a game to get the wiggles out! Create 10 or 20 hopscotch boxes on the floor in a straight line. You can make squares on the floor with painter's tape or go outside and use chalk on the sidewalk or driveway. Have your toddler stand in the middle of the line of boxes. Instruct them to take a certain number of steps forward or back. They could walk the steps or hop the steps! Your toddler will practice listening, following one-step directions, and counting. Mix up the number of steps to keep your child moving. Turn on some music to make it even more fun for your energetic little one!